Published by Creative Education and
Creative Paperbacks
P.O. Box 227, Mankato, Minnesota 56002
Creative Education and Creative Paperbacks
are imprints of The Creative Company
www.thecreativecompany.us

Design by The Design Lab
Production by Chelsey Luther
Art direction by Rita Marshall
Printed in the United States of America

Photographs by Alamy (Redmond Durrell, Nature Pic-
ture Library, Rolf Nussbaumer Photography, Zoonar
GmbH), Corbis (Claus Meyer), Minden Pictures
(Donald M. Jones), National Geographic Creative
(BIANCA LAVIES, MARESA PRYOR), Shutterstock
(Klaus Balzano, VOLYK IEVGENII, Heiko Kiera, My-
Images – Micha, Waddell Images)

Library of Congress Cataloging-in-Publication Data
Names: Riggs, Kate.
Title: Armadillos / Kate Riggs.
Series: Amazing Animals.
Includes bibliographical references and index.
Summary: A basic exploration of the appearance,
behavior, and habitat of armadillos, the distinctively
armored American mammals. Also included is a story
from folklore explaining how armadillos became
musical.
Identifiers: ISBN 978-1-60818-877-2 (hardcover)
/ ISBN 978-1-62832-493-8 (pbk) / ISBN 978-1-
56660-929-6 (eBook)

This title has been submitted for CIP processing under
LCCN 2017011447.

CCSS: RI.1.1, 2, 4, 5, 6, 7; RI.2.2, 5, 6, 7, 10;
RI.3.1, 5, 7, 8; RF.1.1, 3, 4; RF.2.3, 4

First Edition HC 9 8 7 6 5 4 3 2 1
First Edition PBK 9 8 7 6 5 4 3 2 1

ARMADILLOS

BY KATE RIGGS

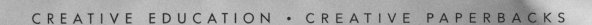

CREATIVE EDUCATION • CREATIVE PAPERBACKS

Armadillos are animals from South America. There are 21 kinds of armadillos. One kind lives in North America. It is the nine-banded armadillo.

The nine-banded armadillo is the most widespread kind

The 3 kinds of hairy armadillos have as many as 18 bands

An armadillo's hard covering is made of bone. There are about 2,000 scales covering the bone. Bands in the middle of the body connect the other parts of the **carapace**.

carapace the hard, bony shell that protects an armadillo's body

Armadillos sleep up to 16 hours a day in their burrows

The legs of an armadillo are short and strong. Sharp claws on the toes are used for digging. Armadillos dig **burrows**. They spend most of the day asleep underground.

burrows holes or tunnels dug in the ground for use as a home

Giant armadillos are about three feet (0.9 m) long. They weigh 70 to 110 pounds (31.8–49.9 kg). Most armadillos weigh 3 to 11 pounds (1.4–5 kg). The smallest kinds are no heavier than five slices of bread!

Nine-banded armadillos can weigh up to 17 pounds (7.7 kg)

Like their anteater relatives, armadillos also have long tongues

Armadillo claws dig for food. Armadillos eat **insects**, spiders, and scorpions. They smell termites inside a mound. They use their sticky tongues to grab the food.

insects small animals with three body parts and six legs

Newborn pups' cara-
paces are soft for the
first few days or weeks

A female armadillo digs a special burrow. She gives birth to one to three **pups** there. Nine-banded armadillo pups are born with open eyes. They are about the size of a stick of butter. All pups stay in the burrow for at least a month.

pups baby armadillos

After two to five months, young armadillos leave their mothers. They look for food on their own. They cannot see well. But their sense of smell is strong.

Armadillos will follow their noses almost anywhere

*Three-banded
armadillos can roll
even tighter to pinch
a predator*

Most armadillos are active at night. They listen for jaguars, snakes, and other **predators**. Some armadillos make loud, squealing sounds. Two kinds of armadillos roll into a ball.

predators animals that kill and eat other animals

Armadillos are shy animals. People try to study them in the wild. In Texas, you can see them many places. These armored animals are one-of-a-kind!

Some kinds of armadillos have fur over their entire bodies

An Armadillo Story

How did armadillos become musical? People in South America told a story about this. Armadillo loved music. He wished he could sing like the frogs and crickets. A musician told Armadillo that his wish would come true. But Armadillo would have to wait a long time. After Armadillo lived a long and happy life, he died. The musician made his shell into a beautiful instrument. Armadillo sang at last.

Read More

Meister, Cari. *Armored Animals*. Minneapolis: Jump!, 2016.

Schuetz, Kari. *Armadillos*. Minneapolis: Bellwether Media, 2012.

Websites

Enchanted Learning: Armadillos
http://www.enchantedlearning.com/subjects/mammals/armadillo/Armadilloprintout.shtml
This site has more information about armadillos and a picture to color.

San Diego Zoo Kids: Three-Banded Armadillo
http://kids.sandiegozoo.org/animals/mammals/3-banded-armadillo
Learn more about the armadillo that can roll itself into a ball.

Note: Every effort has been made to ensure that the websites listed above are suitable for children, that they have educational value, and that they contain no inappropriate material. However, because of the nature of the Internet, it is impossible to guarantee that these sites will remain active indefinitely or that their contents will not be altered.

ARMADILLOS